Periplum *and other poems*

PETER GIZZI grew up in Pittsfield, Massachusetts. His poetry collections include *Artificial Heart* (Burning Deck, 1998) and *Some Values of Landscape and Weather* (Wesleyan, 2003). In 1994 he received the Lavan Younger Poet Award from the Academy of American Poets. He is also the editor of *The House That Jack Built: The Collected Lectures of Jack Spicer* (Wesleyan, 1998). He teaches at the University of Massachusetts at Amherst.

Also by Peter Gizzi

Some Values of Landscape and Weather (Wesleyan, 2003)
Artificial Heart (Burning Deck, 1998)

Periplum
and other poems

1987–1992

PETER GIZZI

SALT

CAMBRIDGE

PUBLISHED BY SALT PUBLISHING
PO Box 937, Great Wilbraham, Cambridge PDO CB1 5JX United Kingdom
PO Box 202, Applecross, Western Australia 6153

© Peter Gizzi, 1992, 1994, 2004

The right of Peter Gizzi to be identified as the
author of this work has been asserted by him in accordance
with Section 77 of the Copyright, Designs and Patents Act 1988.

First published by Avec Books, 1992
Second edition, 2004

Printed and bound in the United Kingdom by Lightning Source

Typeset in Swift 9.5 / 13

ISBN 1 84471 073 4 paperback

SP

1 3 5 7 9 8 6 4 2

Contents

I. PERIPLUM

Song of the Interior Begin — 3
Mahler's 2nd — 4
Mise en Scène — 5
Periplum — 6
The Locket — 7
News at Eleven — 8
Hierophant — 10
The Creation — 11
The Locket — 13
Periplum II — 14
Life Continues — 15
Conceit — 17
Song of the Comparative Night — 18
The Locket — 19
Periplum III — 20
The Locket — 21
Hubris — 22
Song of a Lexicon — 23
Periplum IV — 24
Blue Peter — 25
A.K.A. — 28
Song of the Liver — 29
The Locket — 30
Periplum V — 31
The Locket — 32

Nocturne   33
Song : I Lost My Pail   34
Periplum VI   35
Despite Your Notices   36
Capital   38
Song of the Den   39
Deus ex Machina   41
Song of an Acute Angle   44
The Locket   45
Periplum VII (a valentine)   46
A.K.A.   47
Hard as Ash   48

II. MUSIC FOR FILMS
Music for Films   59

III. OTHER POEMS
Hours of the Book   101
Nostos : Pro Patria   109
Thirty Sentences for No One   110
Psalm   111
Poem for John Wieners   112
Postcard : I Hear America Singing   114
Façades for Theron Ware   115
Often I Am Allowed These Messages   120
Dear Jack   122
Asserted Abundance   124
Still Life with Automobile   125
A Speaking Part   126

Acknowledgements

Grateful acknowledgement is made to the editors of the following journals in which these poems first appeared: *Avec, Cathay, Clerestory, Conjunctions, Dark Ages Clasp the Daisy Root, Five Fingers Review, Grand Street, The Impercipient, Le cahier du refuge, New American Writing, o•blēk, The Painted Bride Quarterly, Screens & Tasted Parallels, Talisman, Tyounyi,* and *Up Rising.*

Thanks also to the editors of the following anthologies in which some of these poems appeared: "Mahler's 2nd," *Broadway* 2, edited by James Schuyler and Charles North, New York: Hanging Loose Press, 1989; "Compline," On CD-ROM, read by Thomas Dolby, *The Invisible Universe,* edited by Fiorella Terenzi, New York: Janus Films/Voyager Press; "Poem for John Wieners," "News at Eleven," "Life Continues," "Deus Ex Machina," *An Anthology of New (American) Poets,* edited by Lisa Jarnot, Chris Stroffolino, and Leonard Schwartz, Jersey City: Talisman House, 1998; "Poem for John Wieners," *The Blind See Only this World,* edited by William Corbett, Michael Gizzi, and Joe Torra, Boston: Pressed Wafer, 2000.

Many thanks to the editors and presses where these works first appeared in book form: Cydney Chadwick for *Periplum,* Penngrove: Avec Books, 1992. Gale Nelson for *Music for Films,* Providence: Paradigm Press, 1992. Manuel Brito for *Hours of the Book,* Gran Canaria: Zasterle Press, 1994.

The epigraph for the poem "Hard as Ash" is from an unattributed quote in Joan Retallack's essay "Non-Euclidean Narrative Combustion

(Or What the Subtitles Can't Say)," in *Conversant Essays: Contemporary Poets on Poetry*, ed. James McCorkle, Wayne State University Press, Detroit, 1990.

Music for Films takes its title from Brian Eno's compositions of the same name.

Thanks also to Eric Baus, Sueyeun Juliette Lee, Nick Moudry, and Rebecca Rosen for manuscript preparation.

I. Periplum

I cannot live with You —
It would be Life—
And Life is over there—
      — EMILY DICKINSON

Orpheus was never really threatened by the Underworld during his visits there. In this poem they present him with a diplomatic note.
      — JACK SPICER

Song of the Interior Begin

Some sky of hydraulic
spring   Some season ever
So the tree for even
a twig   O branch   O earth

there is too   (psalm)
Neither a pool nor
a crown   And day spills
to where is   O water

Begin! Begin! So sing
of lever   Are eyes
shy?   O iris   O onyx
Into blouse of

      Air go there!

Mahler's 2nd

In the beginning was the worm and the worm
turned to sod. It is the spring
that undoes winter which quilted is quiet
light building in solitary procession.
One block of lead after the other moving
in an endless array of grey tho humorless
is worn demurely which is the custom.

Only spring is listless myth. Myopic
ecstasy with nether earth, for a keepsake
is a rainy day a wishing well in afternoon.
A hand becoming an object portends a translation,
an artifact only dust will embrace intimately.
Say when does the phallus become a prick ?

The river moves. We are moved. This is
not uncommon our momentary communion with
house, mountain, water is all ours to transcend
as we arrive. This spring is chilled
awakening to touch these tendons
moving a darker reluctance into blossom.
Inescapable cant of the axis/heart.

Mise en Scène

Not knowing the name for something
proves nothing.

—JAMES SCHUYLER

The shortest distance between
two points is around the world,
and commerce is a word we can
appropriate to use here, but more
than this it is our achievement
of evening silence. A scarf
billowing, draped upon a door latch
in fragrant air. Vulnerable is
another word to attach to this
opening, a vivisection I fill
with eyelash teeth. Although
there was no piano to state the theme
there is music in our night space.
Breath making skin upon ribs taut.
That the formal alphabet of silence
(with or without a future) reveals
a language of the spine and sphinx
of wrists and ankles. Hair blue
black in china braids embellishes
this setting. In the book of my
archaeology your rib cage means
everything, because for years
absence has been my collarbone,
and I a sorry borderguard of this
sad state. Yes, an invisible X marks
the spot where you touch me,
right here, between wanting
and understanding between revelation
and the secret. This intersection
at the extremes of our walk.

Periplum

Put your map right with the world

The person who knows where
has made an accurate study

of here

As to know
implies a different reading

Somewhere

faith enters
and must be pinned and sighted

A church tower is good for reference
but losing ground

Still

satellites orbiting the earth
track a true arc

but perhaps too grand
for everyday distances

And never mind about the bewilderment

"I'm at sea"

The Locket

After the holiday the phone was
silent, and the deserted station.

When a face, static with grief,
looks beyond. Roll over.

Play dead. Try to forgive the
events that follow. To separate

this day and pure emotion
into office hours or a hot meal.

Finally to see that *W* written
across the horizon. Rising

above the houses as evening wore
on. Indelible. Winking out there.

And the wide shore just a hem
full with wind, or laughter, though

the food was good those days
in single file. In solemn rows.

Adding a new grave every seven
rods from the navel. In any

direction unable to distinguish a smile
from a scar. And this accounting.

News at Eleven

The treatment of the missing fare
will not account for absence
equated on the astrolabe of memory.
This in itself some achievement
of unnamed organs of discourse,
like a hippogriff in dreams
on wet lawns of Saturday eve
with Betty and Veronica, such pastel
impossibilities in adolescent moonlight.
Walking the boulevard through the years
you arrive always here about to depart
and going return for the lastings
and stayings of reflexive reveries.
Although time past will become a new
setting in the parlor, recalling
the light of a passing day's impression,
played severely upon the ceiling.
Night meditations of personal
adventure. So let's go back to
that sunlit beach or to rivers
and mountains if you prefer
a device, then one will be fashioned
to employ all the colors of that
faded photograph with what's his name
laughing so intently in the moment.
But it is precisely not that moment
with which you adhere, and tracking
the affect there is another event
with its own colors and agenda,
sounds from which your present gestures
are drawn to try with words, to infuse
a specific feeling, though displacement

follows your every so-called denouement.
So return to the glow of the television
and car horns outside
that startle only for an instant,
though the message is closer to
those sirens, the ones you wake
to in the periphery of sleep.
"One of our submarines is missing
tonight," and to begin here
is a rope looking for an end.
Conclusion may be convenient
if not altogether catastrophic.
This report is inadequate,
no graph to illustrate a fear
escalating beyond, any rational
notion of belief, systems
to produce the intangible
dividend of change, an address
of one state to the next residence.
The house uncommon in its foundation
is set precariously out on a limb
or latest whim to inspire
a feeling of security, an operation
of trompe l'oeil employed at all the seams
to appear invisible.

Hierophant

Automatic is a sentence
from a past conversation
without a future

language is atmospheric
and a stone
thrown from the irrelevant

to the real

There is only this season
and the missing pomegranate seeds
the myth of childhood happiness
and water dreams
for the body is an instrument

Lost children are really not lost
in the woods
you come upon an enthusiast
her name is a labyrinth
she will affix petals to your lips
saying "bad magic is a false tooth
bearing bad blood to your heart."

no bramble of myrtle . . .

The lost child in the grimm forest
The body is a compass made of cork
and a pin floating in a glass bowl

The Creation

There are two rooms and a door

She is speaking a telling and a pause

There is the world known and otherwise

One room for paintings

Her story is a telling of the fall of water

Her story against theirs is

Here is where her telling lies

The painting of a woman preparing her toilet

This painting against a white field

Between these rooms a history

We walked the hill in autumn

She gave me her hand we looked at the building

Food took place between the rooms and our walk

Intervals for food for walks for paintings

Her story was a telling against the sky

Her telling is where my story lies

The painting was not a story

The painting was not a telling and a pause

The painting was and is for now

Her story was now and now here

Food was introduced as the control

There are two things then three certainly more

Simultaneous history is telling

The breath and beat of the thing

The thing being a history of this world

Between the walks and door

The Locket

Here is the ashtray and here
the plastic cup of cool water.

And here is the known world.
As fingers duplicate the event

of hunger. Get up. Go
to the division of various

stories and look for the naked
man beneath the stream

behind the house. The same
house that *I* does not inhabit.

The car is there. The letters
are there. And this street

leads to no particular day.
The way home remains

a mystery to those who are
looking. How else recover

what otherwise is. Lost
to the open. Space between

leaves and stones. Here
also is the neighborhood.

Periplum II

"My pain is not physical
but slow languish of sentences"

you said
Baroque as any attempt

to conceal

yet another night
endured

The room was now opened
ungrammatical as

A heart

consistent and
indifferent

a brio for the tenuous and time
will not relinquish even an hour

Let alone now

Life Continues

Life continues while the telephone intersects continuity with another party. The day will occur with or without your approval, though to get you on the wire and arrange a meeting is sunny. A forecast of hope has provided excitement this afternoon. No, a forecast of excitement has provided hope this afternoon.

The world happens at your doorstep. There is no method to decipher this day. The birds and the bees are both moving geometric patterns. To connect one plain with another horizon. There are doors everywhere we walk and occasionally stumble upon a carcass, which now is only a frame—the door is ajar. This place once marked an exit. Today it is a wall. Where is the magician of openings?

To question the infinite is an inarticulate gnarl, better to blur at the humidity of touching. Love, I stopped by to pitch some woo, we walked to town in Chinese shoes. There are doors into which we can enter, to move through this room, indecision and terror. That the light is blinding over there or the darkness here is without hospitality is beyond my calling, though limbs answer and bear solace for a space called imaginary time. There is no measure of year or day let alone now held in these arms. Time kept on a clock whose hands are beautiful, to say you, here, or there you are, is irrelevant to this field of stars. The night yields repose of the unknown, for the physical has no identity, is why we close our eyes when we touch one another, and this one is felt upon the flanks of my body's shivering and released at the nape. Only how to resolve this face before me? Facing the horizon of my shoulders.

Bless *you*. The you now here in italics, the you of the ways, you of the aquamarine, you with the oasis touch, you of the pandering smile, you with a greasy heart, you lacking denouement, you of heroic conceits, you who forgot, you who did not awake, you who awoke and cannot forget, you of the suicides, you with murdering hands, you of the carbuncle gaze, you who will die, you who will not die, you blush, you blur, you in the figure of a question mark, you are, this *you*, you too and you and you and you.

Conceit

> the heart uselessly opens
> to 3 words
> — GEORGE OPPEN

Who are you to transpose sorrow's term
to a tracing of this hand on that mouth.

Saying:
"Here is my heart,
there is the world."

I will follow this sentence to the sun.

In the eye of the solar plexus
breath hungers.
An atavistic forecast.

Your touch

starts at the surface
of the world and sounds
to synapse music.

The arc of my nerve alive with your salt.

Song of the Comparative Night

Your hydrogen smile dissolves me.
Tips my thermometer to an impossible
    centigrade. C'mere.
My dowser's wand is more atomic
    than sunshine when you're near.
The invisible gears of earth mesh
    at the base of my want,
when supplication becomes a whimper
    without a bang!
You are hydro-electric power and
    that turbine of night out there
reminds me of the hydraulics of hips
    and eyes I call your big combo.
I am blacker than a new moon in winter.

The Locket

Dear E. Who was that thin
figure inhabiting a bedroom?

This substitution of language.
Will never escape the alibi

it produces. Wrinkled and
pink as the new day out

the dirty kitchen window.
The skull is new too where-

as the heart is dirty. Unruly
curtain of desire and death.

This is certainly not done
to obtain a mastery of tone.

The soloist lives inside notes.
These glad parades of children

wind down to a fine powder.
Reach to the deep grin floating

on the surface of the lake.
All pinafores are sad in rain.

Then there can't become the
pronoun it was hoping to say.

Periplum III

A laundry list and chores

but the sentence continues
to keep house

An egg timer instructs

and startled
the approach failed

Pacing frantically increases energy
but to what end

of the room will yield hospitality

The pineapple was halved
and ready

or as the narrative continues
Open

for any reading

The Locket

All the mirrors in the world
or all the world mirrors and

won't help. The small boy
walking home from school

alone. The lawns now deep
green and alive with beetles.

The song is imprinted in the
season as faint as a cloud.

Or a hand reaching to heaven.
Dusk brushing against the five

promises of growing up into
the world or these houses. A

future perfect with meals and
television in the den. Then

a bough breaks and the cradle
spills into a backyard

where families are. Tethered.
And faded pennants of a Maypole.

And there are fissures too small and
too many, everywhere, to find Y.

Hubris

Grief is a rut
I'm quick to furnish
A frieze of dust and tears
And the garden is abortive
Lawn chairs (empty)
Clank under a leaded sky
Spring's a heavy
While
The reflecting pool
Only a surface without consideration
Others sink to this music
As I double-clutch into the ozone

The room I inhabit (dada)
Is mottled and water-stained
These ruins are my champions
Sword strokes into air cut deep
And to trade wounds for words
Here
I'm afraid I won't return
And the winds ask "who are
you saving your kisses for?"
This architecture prevents closure
And I seek protection
From another morning's weaponry
I am hiding
As who abstracts into a god

Song of a Lexicon

It is not simple to say
      zero
this my double
and I equals the letters
      of my name

Darling if I come to you
as a selfish word
as dry pages in a book
      break my temper
and drown these spooks

It is only this house
      we enter
a difficult tenure
when others loiter

behind a library
      a vacant sign

Periplum IV

He did not want
to hide

in or out of the narrative

but vocabulary left him
down to the roots

of what might have flourished

A handful of forget-me-nots
insisted

to foreground this

He fixed an owl to the center
of his mission

Now was only left
to voice

this terrible stare

Blue Peter

To describe a logic of sight
pull the surface onto target and
arrive at zero aperture. Then
fluctuate to a face, reproduced
in serial format, superimposed
upon marginal pedestrians,
traversing a polarity of earth.

The axis here is askew, perhaps
unsettling, the way physical
equilibrium slides into multiple
perspective. This place where
sight informs the eye as gate
to phenomenon, a bridge to
impulse the imaginary. Simply

she was feeding bread to pigeons
in the park. So begin this sentence
with rain and square the surrounding
flat with common traffic. I
move through, to get here. If you
want me, you will find me in
the garden of vestiges, next to

the sweet water cistern. Where
the old port remains, a water
mark on granite, abutted with
grass and a stone path leading
to other places that for the moment
I am not interested in, as I take
serious your claim to provoke you.

And I will follow your instructions,
however silly, however sublime, until
you have found me, indistinguishable
from what you call, your self.
The way I wear you about my
mouth, as a crease, deepening
every time I smile to look at you.

Look at me. I'm serious, I must
find the way, to say, we have arrived.
For it is you who instruct me in
the laws of perspective, these many
converging lines, drawn to perception.
So that I have become only a star or
an asterisk or a compass rose. Signifying

location, this possibility of place. True.
It's been said that the burial of the dead
is the beginning of culture, as we know,
no other. And I remain raw.
Vapor digit tapping at my wrist,
the talon, the dorsal fin and the panther
claw. The value of negative space

and the rationale of talisman does
not parse, will not parry from this
dearth. As emotions surround the edge
of the planet adjusted to actual people we meet.
What could the difference of this construction
intend in a world of moments, merely
fragments provided to express conversation

or random noise signaling grey space,
to be inserted within an imported structure?
Birds migrate over cityscape and arrive
in my backyard to a mutiny of peaceful
dawn. Then a description of equality
is scored, as a rhetorical flourish is installed
for testimony. I flag. I stammer.

A banner to the burden that all things
that are, must not be, in me. Only,
will you not smile when I wave?

A.K.A.

I wanted beauty, was given endurance.
My features too loud to fit in a compact.
Contact sports and bruises would do for rouge.
Perfumed, my heart was chiffon with a string
      of pearls for secrets.
Then the straps of this mantle gave way and fell
    like a camisole to my ankles.
Exposing this posture.
The prodigal son eats at Burger King, sabotaged
      from birth with sugar and a baseball cap.

Run around   run the bases
      run away   run down.

A missing cuff-link falls from space onto the carport.
We're dressing for the movies.
I live elsewhere. I'm growing home.

Song of the Liver

I was trying to remove the splint
from my smile, while the moon
sank into the funhouse mirror.
Gee, can songs do that to the night?

I was trying to recover the sighs
of my hands, then the sun
threw a tongue across my back.
Could this be the hour of the clock?

I was trying to recapitulate the parks
in my spine, as the earth
rose to this lump in my costume.
Now I can never hide again?

What was the lesson of the flower
      and will I go there alone?

Who will resolve me of my shame?
      O shadow! O scythe!

The Locket

Stay there 0 and forgive
the usages known as speech.

Called a declaration, called a
pilgrim stave from the father's

house. Organ of the other
senses. A phantom anthem.

Smoke signals interpreted
by cities built on a rising

plain. Intimate talk on
the stoops of the inward

city, without occupation. A
blue sky between pedestrians.

Horizon time. And empty
hours collect on paper.

Ink of the present. Stain
of the present. This then; is

where; to begin. An old
calendar names the day,

but what name is given
to provide against a past?

Periplum V

Vision longed
to shelter these many

late nights

where the past gives
No telling

could suffice the agony to wend

and the ellipsis was complete
A geographical stop

in the terrestrial instrument

I don't give a 'hoot'
A voice as weird as a wind splint

escaping

despite an elaborate overlay
A line of poetry

The Locket

Next the composition insists
on playing the game for keeps.

Children report news for-
gotten from a field in April.

Not the second person singular
but a U written on bark. To be

replaced to a different location.
Known, as a life. A label is applied.

Then removed when all else fails
as all else does. Warning.

This description follows an
indefinite article. Transpose

a yellow ball for a red bike.
No better for the objects.

A siren, a bell, a car horn,
a hand, a house, a cigarette

burning, a meal, a table,
a clock, a steeple, a cat,

a transparent blouse. The noise,
the transistor, and the radio on.

Nocturne

The day is an abandoned article.
In this miscellany I cannot
find a way to speak.
To say water lights at eventide
is seamless. Indecipherable
cause that extends out
the window to steeple
leads to lip stain.
Having been in your mouth
I walk the finger of the sundial
home and bruise the winter skyline
to psalm. The day goes to ground
as the sun drags over antique hills
with only a memory of heat burning
in another quadrant of the brain.
And as for beauty—don't say it.
The day is down and I dismount.

Song: I Lost My Pail

You break my gong.
Bust my crock.
Blur all the stops.

Your thin has meaning
to me, thighs so long
to be starlight, release me.

You blush of a deeper wafer.
You wand me up beauty.

O Atthis who fingers
your smile as my moon
wanes outside the ego

outside my hamlet. This
little sandbox for a clumsy
heart. Over here. Over

there. No way of even
or being "kind" about this.

Periplum VI

To embark too young as yet
for foresight

blazing a trail
through pathless tracts

I maintain

insubstantial shapes
thrown from the surface

Cicadas for instance shed tubular jackets
periodic of summer

activity

The same way our doctrine often seems misplaced
and you study chemistry

to put some depth in the field
Where impact occasions

we catch a glimpse

In this context messages wash up
from the dead

letter office

Despite Your Notices

This is my poem. The one I was afraid to show you. A poem to provide against the voices that will ultimately ensure my failure in this endeavor. This poem is a pillow, small and embroidered, the satin death pillow used to prop up the face for one last viewing. All attempts of understanding finally and thoroughly erased. This is my poem. The one I tuck under my eyelids when looking inhibits the distinctions of what can be seen. And air always present, always there to stimulate the hair at the base of my neck. Insert this chill exactly where you presume to have found me, only to uncover an abandoned parking lot for eyes. Look harder and you will discover we are all matched to this swatch of steel grey that is as wide as the seam on my scrotum but longer than the chalk ray on the board in the classroom to represent infinity. Silent and irreversible. A fault line running from one hole to another. Forever. That we are drawn, together. So see you on the other side. Even if we can't represent that which we were hoping to resemble. But for one day heaven. See the tips of buds swaying in union beneath a spring sky so faint so blue that it could only suggest a further devastation, as if we were fated to repeat this day, as if we could. It came and went without the anxiety of anticipation and its finality of passage and unannounced significance stains us good. Even the colors fade so we can only imagine we were once so alive. Sad nothing can be held so thoroughly we might assimilate it. Only in the letting go will the full concentration of tone bleed into the periphery of our lives and settle into a patina that can never be altered. I surrender my vision thus. Because I don't understand. That joke isn't funny anymore. It cuts me precisely where laughter is a departure from this parlor. I live on flight 405 departing into an icy altitude—cold and detached. I'm here despite your notices and obituary. That plane didn't crash. It still hovers around my head. The constant hum of its engines reminds me I still haven't landed. I know this by the way a hand like a landing strip will reach over to wave here, here, here. So here again is the earth. Not the idea of it, but that clump of dirt and weeds outside my door each day—humiliates me. So long. I'm off to my job, alone in the clouds where my fathers live perhaps younger than I am now. Having left me to dinners, movies, books and with this incredible sickness you call enthusiasm. It's a smoke screen though. For it was me they stuck out there in that winter hole. Earth so frozen it came up in slags that still get caught in my throat every time you tell me you love me. So don't. I mate with these voices on the other side. Their memos become the mottos of my solo walk into emblem. As the torn metal of all industrial accidents flowers in my brain. Yeah, I saw the broadcast. Transmission deceived.

Capital

A woman wearing a surface
on an avenue with any name

This is where I live?
So I'll see you later

Explore the possibility of form
and we arrive at common denominator

What does this tell you
that I don't already grow

By the time of disputes
a smile renews an ambiguity

Back to the shining truth
of possible loins and precise

A dictionary of exact forgeries
ruins of a posthumous integer

I refuse the yoke and buckle
Say, what movie were we watching?

As I am reminded of my pinky
useless and that it is mine

And because today is Friday
you expand in the folds of my pocket

Song of the Den

The small heart
opens out
to meet the world

it carries news

of kindness
for there is only
this and

these small hands
offering
the weather

My street is
not the same
since we've met

and darker
for goodbye

The fierce
life is quiet

tenacious as
a parlor for one
where people are

an effort
outside

the walk
to your house
is mirrored

at night
out my window
the crowded

sky

Deus ex Machina

I guess if we get to be here today
and watch this movie together
it has all been worth these past thirty odd years
it took to get here
on this Tuesday. In this city.
Is why I'm here. To know you.
I will compare knowing and saying
and tell of all such coordinates
that run together to the river replete with its ghosts
in this instance of talk.
But we won't scuttle. Will we?
As it gave the first buoy of its name.
Friendship, so entire, so perfect
you will hardly find the like elsewhere.
Even if the buildings are all in disrepair,
please, don't let that inform us.
It's meant for us, to pass by that dogwood tree
in May as our voices carry into Thursday twilight.
May I keep this promise?
Along with those petals flaunting the new season.
Little pennants of time. Boundary stones
to be collected on the periphery, where I live,
and where I remain, so I'll be here thinking of you.
Don't worry. I'll work hard. Places everyone.

When sunlight accumulates in afternoon.
A box of elderberry lists behind the alcove . . .
then description fails the reader and we
are left with only shapes and patterns. Still
a single leaf trembles on the breeze.
Emblematic, a lovely badge, serrated
and at peace with the day that has flowered
beyond the notion of our need.

Where the reader lists. The poet builds a room,
it can be small or grand depending on the tone
as in June her garden is real.
An intricate lace of affection to correspond
when wanting fails. Perhaps a yellowed doily
on your grandmother's nightstand
like a tune, long off, played
on a toy piano. Clink. These lapses
from time to time fill hours and cars
on the highway. A room to include your ramble,
as well as itinerant interlopers visiting
from unforeseen lake districts—with its news
of festival lights and famous contests—
where the song dies down into rotting hulks,
trunks exposed at the sleeve of the shore.
These transitions or seams if you like
inform me. Water and land disguised as matter.
A carcass dressed and open for inspection
revealing nothing but process, lovely and
inescapable from our own play.

I was waiting behind the skene, worn,
ravaged from too many trips to the provinces,
too many performances, too many nights
accosted by the rabble. Some people got a lot a gun.
What makes you different? Show me.
Here's a dime. Call your dead
and find out what they've learned.
Having been too preoccupied with the house
and its metaphors and where
the objects would lead them. Too selfish
to watch out for us. Abandoned,
beautiful and wide-eyed, developing the tools

to maintain the glorious liberties we carry
in our hearts and pockets. Then something
else did come to stand in its place: namely you.
Which is where I'm going tonight,
despite the distance from seam to shadow.
For I am relative to your I, while
this page walks into my side, where
the sun sets. It's a special light this.
When evening takes a sip off the din
of long endurance, becalm, be near me
always—book. So I and I and I we go.
Together under the elms. Won't that be nice?
To watch one by one all the colors
drain out of the sky into our organs.

Song of an Acute Angle

Eros' sling of geometry

I call my shiny
tricorne hat

has got me untoward
has got me

a tattoo

where the bit
retreats into then
ends where now
begins and you

sleeping late

The insect negotiates
a grass blade

where breath is

an eyelid
turning to meet

me turning away

The Locket

This day black knee socks
on a grey field, on a new

page. A few dogs will bark.
Where the yards join the skies.

There is the diagram and no
amount of sleep will erase

the serendipity of kisses.
A smile torn and where

fissures expand on concrete
—little birds shift.

How diligent is protein.
When the plate warms

into a green swath mixed
with evidence of return.

It does not emote anything
except itself. The pale lawn

is the pale lawn, the lesson
of food is that it is food.

Simple. All day the letter
A and nothing else. Ah.

Periplum VII (a valentine)

If I could tell you this
or tell where this is
or where on a given map
this being is
then I would give it to you
though I will not name it
which would not serve
this being the unnamed force
the absolute unnamed this
of our experience together
or to believe that this place
could be made
or if belief could make this space possible
then I will meet you there
live with you there
and discover the essential experience
of being there together
the irreducible together
of this being you
being me
articulate and lithe

A.K.A.

I notice people
and the hands they wear.
Tell me again, whose
hand to god?

Being limited living
in this distance of arms
reach, here where the sky
says only "black" then "blue."

I am savage
like DaVinci's St. Jerome
unfinished and naked.
I am empty. I am
open and nothing could
tell this, my wanting
to be found.

Do not force your hand.
I seek even waters. Maps
don't lead anywhere.
That's it. Geronimo!

Hard as Ash

On September 20, 1938, Miss Newcombe, 22, combusted
before a roomful of people while waltzing in a dance hall in
Chelmsford, England. Blue flames erupted from her body and
in a matter of minutes she was reduced to a small pile of ash.

Some trees cannot grow without fire.
Private catastrophes at the speed of Phaethon.
What was X? Without faith an integer of light broke
into cities of geometry. Define Y.
In the desert it is all calculus. In an overcoat
in winter, without socks I wandered into night.
One by one all the bars fell into place.
The day of the talking stones is
no longer. The dreams of metamorphosis.
The morning you woke up and for a moment forgot
to call them "dead," it was the morning
of the poem. The subject is the content into
which I step lovingly. This lapidary effect
of all sons sets where houses invest
the notions of "home" or "hearth" and heat
gives even as the earth rolls over
into night and is contained or content
to remain itself while still breaking
into flower or streets with cadences of wind.
Your musics insist to inform me by
remaining plastic. With you I will revise
the entire possibility of twilight.
The day is woven into images we adhere to
only memory of light against
a screen door ajar. Then children's
faces appear. A thematic see-saw,
silhouetted now—romantic and real.
How can we say in this hour, who
will resolve the interplay of your countenance,

this ellipsis, the way you come
to me pictorially, in time, with space
that is real. Though someone will die
and I'll have to wear a tie, again.
This is only a poem to say I love you.
I love you too. I've been so happy.
Happy! These sun notes bend the porpoise
in my eye, quiet the pony inside. You know,
when the creek meets the little paper hats
floating out to sea. The cabby goes past
your stop but the bar on the corner
wears a preternatural smile, is more
companionable than what you call home.
So you discover hospitality in tight pants
where the traffic goes both ways.
Has anyone asked you lately
are you all right in your new homes
and does your electric bill depress you
when they cut your powwow?
I was going to build you a flower.
Then the day broke apart. Big leaves
halved and greasy as a waxy stem revealed
a voice I misplaced when I was a girl.
It was summer and we were there
and so was the phonograph
and the missing relatives drowned
earlier in the century during the great migration
of sentences when words were collected
with a winnowing fan. You should have seen it.
I did. Then it was another day arrived
unlike the stubble that had grown up
before, clear and wide with a glint
around all the small names

belonging to the places they are keeping.
When objects become the subject, a veritable
picnic of description that spells glee on the new
horizon. Time is our only subject
and the mutability of forms. Time compact
and out of sight. I want the whole essay.
Collocated with clouds and silver.
Still, sky makes its cinematic sweep over
this burg and to think we get to have coffee
together now and then is pretty terrific
don't you think? I have come to tell
of the discrepancies of light, material
or otherwise. It makes no difference as the meal
went to waste outside on the knoll where
the neighborhood is tucked into the nights.
Rest safely my beloved for I am coming.
I was going about my business, the way I do
and then from nowhere came a fable
to my doorstep and would not let me alone.
Not now. Not ever. This neon winked its
marquee on my forehead and it flashed—true
and good. Not just any good, but good
as in a farmer's prayer about earth
and work and rest. O mommy is it true?
Do these beans grow to the sky?
It is the alphabet lies close to ground.
Broken tile to marvel at and so much emotion
goes into learning to make these letters.
A spell against time. Chumming for clarity
and a pronoun to share. Though twenty-six
sounds are not enough. But what the news
didn't say is she loves her darling Comacho
the darling way he attends her every sob

and whimper. And do not mistake this freedom
for a swagger. My heart was shorn
long before speech and the act itself
overbounds my physical bluster, here
in a body, where an axe splits the wind
from my mouth. This trill at the edge.
Look kids here's the tempo. So pick it up.
The name of this song is new feeling, because
that's what it's about. No monk on a stoop.
I am here. Ask me now.
Saying leave me alone, I am only a poem,
what do you want from me? What do you want
from me teeth? To incise earth? No rest to pillow
my weird. O clack of breeze. I am not abated.
When is a child's bottom lip enough to say—quit it?
This thought bit me the other day. As all
my pictures have fallen but that don't make 'em
go away. Meanwhile there is not an index
or a Cliff note for you, wanting to walk
blankly off into a grove where all punctuation
lists, like you, brilliant in its particularity
and distinction. The grass outside is waving
and alive with protein disguised in so many
colors and shapes that form itself is
the only envelope I await. "God
bless Captain Vere!" Now winnow me
under harbor lights. Who sleeps in the now
of flowers my bed of prince? I capsize into the birth
mark on my thigh. I am marked and can
never be yours, but this allows me to be
eternally deferential. I dream of pulleys
in the sun all day and no water will cleanse
the little stain I wear about my smile.

For shame is my hidden lever to fulcrum
the earth. "How's your gear
Squeak? All in order?" O leaf out my window.
O sky where the tape is blank
and loops. I am sad and strange
in the late morning, in the early afternoon,
in the middle of the night. Yes moon!
My hands shake. Where the distance
of my life is my arm's length. No place
to live I've been told. No place, I've been
told, and still you want to throw me outta
my tent. Having lived among factories
and highways in the nuclear age,
I have learned to pronounce "love"
and to recognize my name written on trees
on rocks in the sky above. Yep, that corn's
straight off the cob, mister. Then it said "I love
Dolores" in white paint against iron
on the rusted trestle. On my way to the heart
of American radio or summer. I was
going to see my friend the human. Do you
understand? When lips kiss and make
a seal, this is the first hermetic doctrine.
I wanna hold your hand. Is there something
I can do now? When the cello bow abrades
my breast will I dissolve finely into air?
Do I have to die for you then to hear these lines
that I make profligate and plaintive for you.
They are parallel lines whose origin is
irretrievable. Each one tells a history.
I remember streets houses trees overhead.
Someone called my name, my dogtag
whistles over here; over there as an adult

I want to thank my family for how I feel
this morning, living under a bridge
scaring children. An unforgivable geometry
insists its repertoire on our dialogue.
Learning to say "my wife my car my color."
I have seen your thin purpose all my life.
So what is an anthem, and growing up there
is a lesson in it. When all forms have been
emptied can I begin? I doubly derive my body.
Running ahead of myself, beyond memory's reach,
the source sprang incarnadine. Teeming
with information. Trembling my standard returned.
I knew then this body was not invincible.
Who shall know this posture, this morning's slide rule.
I needs. I wants. A vista to combat the way
shadow splits and divides on either side
of a pelvic blade. Unity in strict notation.
Dear ghost. Dear reader. I have seen you.
And this at least is one definition, I include,
to become, who I call, myself. A remembrance
got on autumn footpath scurrying on our way
to life. So now when I line up and belong
to persons next to me, I'll be good and eat
my soup. But I'm sick. Sharing real food.
It's getting harder to say now, this
exploded present, doubling back moebius
style on your gaze and the air thick
with tongues. You'll say it's too discursive.
But I have learned more from chicken soup
than all the bright contests. So praise
the retarded man serving me coffee
at the meeting, he has a place. Bless him.
And you think I'm kidding.

What did you do today for someone? Or rather
what have I done to sit here. Call me Dismal.
I wake up a thousand times a day. And ask
three questions. Are you shy are you lost
are you blue? Is there nothing left for you?
Only on holiday or for one holiday only?
From boneyard to schoolyard. All the good
it does you now. Waiting in a parking lot.
O pioneer your keel has run aground,
your stars have betrayed you.
There is no instruction for this light,
no room bigger than a lung. Who can say
in common speech what the crowds were cheering for.
Rushing in at the edges of the map
lamenting the end of the forest. Open the theater,
place the ring inside. A curtain of birds
and fish. A curtain of trees and hills
and vistas. Now bring about words to heal.
Sentences to bring about change. Grammar
that shall inhibit evil? Now: clap hands.
Father tell me what you think
of me. Is it a face or a factory? Come here
to distinguish the burden of a smile. Attached
to lightning. As the world was revealed then returned
to your sandwich. I am who sent me.
Obvious and otherwise a trope was. This laundry
line strung from year to year reaches
to the woman I am becoming. Always leads to my fear.
The difficulties of ambiguity. Or your smile
chosen. A vehicle that allows no passage beyond,
but the surface is bright. You're wrong about clarity,
blue inescapable blue. Not a red sky at night.
What delight can I afford? Though

this might be leading nowhere. This is
a composite map leading me to the horizon
of afternoon, where the you is not erased
or blown away but remains coal ash intact
at the bottom of my mouth. A music
to enhance our margin plotting to broaden
this plain. My field of reference larger than.
To unfold stillness, and giving time time,
I learned to trust the history of my own backyard.
To this day I don't read newspapers.
After all the sun we had. At twilight a salamander
will appear in the core of the reactor.
The day I gave my wedding dress away.

II. Music for Films

for Kent Jones

It should have the greatest possible mobility in order to record
the most fleeting harmony of atmosphere.
— F. W. MURNAU

As if I were only a flower after all and not the map of the country
in which it grows.
— JOHN ASHBERY

Music for Films

the tear and breath
devouring of girl and granite

they breeze to zero
withstanding street

    +

day persists on paper
as twinning evaporates

the rule of again
play of the new one

    +

upon an active surface of blue
bearing day
disintegrating shoal of sky

      ripples
      foliage ripples

swart touches down
touching petals

a blind man

+

space with tremor of night
every opening and close

vanish
inner vicinity
rumors
        and dawn

+

rush to the circle rising
fresco of the many layers
sleeve of water in half-light
veneer absolved of red and yellow
translucent color of soil

+

empty of speech
empty of wind
husk
in the dimming
or time after time
my own
possibility
            of form

+

clay descending slides
cantilevered ray
settles beneath the surface of another pool
an arena
                dilates

difficult candor
belonging to itself

+

withstanding
as actual patterns
ungather

build this mote
and preserve the light

+

beyond a path
sidereal observances
and the anti way
cuts into this plain

+

a web to extend throughout
as a fire expands

sky and shelter arc tremble
a vista cut into the agate blue

take a breath
fall
twinned

+

of the absent agent
prevails

a sneaker squeaks
on an empty street
good-bye
too much to carry

+

to arrive here
says
begin to die

as time erases
a sky radiates colors
throughout

a spine

+

chemical wash
liquid mineral
this means
you are here

and make of it
or else a mirrored alphabet

+

to participate without
consent
of the blood cell
traveling in silence

coded

to perceive open
reverting the impossible
moment
            of breath

+

daybreak to salt charge
behind the eyes
register
        real fire

along the horizon
nothing conflagrates

+

mirage
of the recognitions
the voice as mystery
manipulated
from a disappearing center

+

standing naked
as wanting to atone
for a white edge
against a blue arc
where she walks a path
away from daylight

+

violation of space
is this
tightening web of tendons

bone of another

+

winnow
as the seed expands
return
from the ten thousand folds

or forgotten petals

+

toss the sheaves of longing
upon an open wound
as air's system slides by
an iris
        opening

+

you say flower
as understanding

pretend to understand
and the given
roots commingle
benign is
the force and the way

+

a bruise develops
from a breech in wanting

and form from
disparate weeds makes a tapestry

     for eyes

+

the surface of bright
shines
within chosen smiles
and belongs to a darker limit

+

a reflection
in a night window
where the silence is telling
no thing

the way language is
transparent

+

an apparatus of leaves
collocated into an album
of sensation
where children embrace us

and aging hands
the night tree is androgynous

+

bare and broken
breath in
            tones

to a deity
long forgotten
to eyes
            deciphering

+

but here
you will know me
and from another

      eyes finding

belong to a wind
simple as a child's dress
wavering
not unlike this locust leaf
dancing
          upon the hollow

gutter of a civilization

+

and the voice
replies
a report from glacial shifting
to living's resistance

we are here and must
mean these hands

+

     or else

a message transmitted
to empty palms
the way a mirror
holds us
        to silence

+

silence within lives
the teeming meaning gleaned
annealed
from a broken tongue
broken song

I was telling the real

+

as approach of
afternoon
had your mouth
about it

+

irrepressible sounding
of an immaculate throat
speaks
smooth stones

where ruby was a name
for showing

+

the other
lists

a cat kneading
on a belly of leisure
electric coat
blushing
against an exposed nipple

+

a phantom linger
where muscles thicken

        this apex

allows a prism of green

[70]

+

green thick
and precise as laughter
response of nothing

in particular
explains we have arrived

+

the dangers of frontier
seeming an instance

a new hill has been achieved

+

earth still
if achieved remains
without toil or without impression

a foot pad
on a pine needle floor

+

what could this mean
to apprehend air
and become

    static

vain to consider
the appearance of things

+

a simple fabric drapes
and cleaves

+

there are streets and parlors
more specifically in private
places
there is an idea

unable to communicate
here
    or here

+

a sun shaft remains

and plays an enduring game
wild hare in notation

meanwhile the machine
of the heart

+

betwixt time
space
and an approach of day

earth
        silent

as a sun is
not the only star

+

at dawn
the courtyard opens

night spills
out beyond a cornice

and building
a prayer and this shadow

waxes out of proportion

+

the length of the temporal
interval
immeasurable integer of houses
bristling on the afternoon boulevard

a point becomes darkest
when recognition is full
and shadows converge

+

no sound from shadow
only geometry

explain this phenomenon
of triangles
on a wall
        in june

+

and all breath
receives
as no one
owns the breeze

+

the garden
grows free from possessive
nouns

what name means
              the real

+

light continues
to grow

+

to expose language

become pumice
become dust and
inconclusive is

matter

+

steps where no body
shows
imparts no plan

only the paradigm

+

a dying form

I say sky
as sky remains
the only
means
to admit the void

+

an actual road to dusk
culmination of holes

this taut line of rose
expands
in the moment of night

+

i.e. activity
percolates
as the center dark

devours our past
ajar
falls away

+

in sleep fathoms
a life fierce

as flowers dissipate
an axe blade

+

nearing a caesura

    flight

+

an apparition descends
hearing a storm
distance seems concrete

+

every point
terminates
into the infinite

shadows
your hands play

+

the body atmosphere
is full
pyramids existing
given a base

say your shoulder

+

stay your eyes

an object
transmitted through all

+

space
and in every direction

an acute converging
past
straight lines of a surrounding

air

+

asleep on a divan
fate
no more no less
than a girl

is real

+

breeze
night window
street
leaves become

pyramids
of a smaller
order

+

how else cast the inexorable
breath
small and alive

+

at my flank
the invisible
image of instance

reflects
each other

        endlessly

+

a dahlia stirs
beneath a window shade

+

a dark chamber
by the small space
within an iris

    evolves

an overturned word
ungathers
silence in the emblem
of ruin

+

each body
by itself

everywhere and on all sides
memory
at the speed
      of reflex

+

breath prevails
abrades
my heart narrowingly

a face waves

+

tears
tied with rain

a star is joined
to the lintel

+

this then
is the deconstruction
of a school house

plays about
where fog banks down
to a fine powder

+

quartz

from the same hill
two rapid formations
patrolling wire borders
these events in dense

      fog

+

large the sky
has lost its signal
flare of the interior

      nerve

not a measured room

+

all day some trees
some trees
and slow water

as the grey was mistaken
for a sparrow

+

the resolve
of unmoving duration

or an open field

+

in a library
a song speaks of origin
shining resentment
lost on a shelf

forgotten breath

+

refusal of place
and the distance of four fingers breadth

is smaller than space
between

two eyes

+

and interferes with the sign

of itself
which was magic and there is
responsibility of the household
grown up on
hence
             it is morning

        +

as all branches
of a river
if of equal speed
are equal to the main

body
in question
begins reciprocity
of all limbs having

             a direction

        +

heliotrope

+

again let us
say heliotrope
and an inner whir or knowing

exhibited
in the russet of an eye
materials here are arranged

wherefore thou
who do not know

      this law

+

a hollow forms and develops
to combust with
a noun

a weather seen then taken
away

+

to list to resemble
film
and a central axis
baroque as a forest

[86]

a sequence settles
at the back of the neck

    and grows

+

small talk issued from a wind splint

begin to say here as you
mean to be in this
space
occupied
and yet

    another

+

I was telling
the real

the maple tree
a widow's watch
cornice and column

+

night
tremble light in squares
means neighborhood

and the emptiness
here is the watch tower
and a resting bell

+

this was all
and no more

        there

appears when the return
eddies
of wind be thou
made virtual
                made man

+

dew of the pages made
dusk real and a moon

say jonquil
say bones

and this garden

    a night garden

  +

immeasurable envelope
and an empty hand

reach to water

  +

this is meant to represent
the earth
and her waters vast

moves underground
behind the iris
from the utmost depths

    water

+

and again wet

define first what
is seen
height or depth

+

chance be wind
be the agent of notion
as the ellipse of this sphere
stains floorboards
yellow and ivory

sorrow too spills through this window

+

and green mixes in
mixes
into all
colors belonging

to breath

for there is earth
inside
and to dig

as the day transpires

    +

here was a calm
here a gale arrival
and did not bear

    knowledge

did not instruct
in every tongue
and the song was in
                vented

    +

o where do we go when we go
now here

you are where
an eye opens where
a star awakens here

+

as the same
has abandoned this
delineation of soil and bone

    remains

no third of any
thing
let a be the sun
and m ruffled water

as x is an earth

+

hush
a passing

the poplar leaves
make a shadow gate
ephemeral and perfect

+

these hands threads woven

fine and fitted
for a life

and no more

+

wave of lilies
outside
the doorjamb

vital the breast
of songbirds
hop and shift

+

hop and shift
new thought
stirs on the sidewalk

patterns elaborate
sooth
an eye distracted

+

radiance
of the so many
reflections
transmitted
            to an I

these shadows of the imperceptible
life
endure

            beyond recall

+

5 fingers
4 limbs
2 eyes
and a name

sapiens

by implication
a universe
here
say here

and see

+

a discourse is not place

as blood can be seen
issuing from the torn
flesh
        of man

+

the earth as a world
an image of the sun

as the pool of blood
that lies
about the heart is
an ocean

+

moves about
and dissolves in the eye

the flower transfigured

quick selves ascend to peace
a handful of dirt
as sacrament

+

beginning with a theory
of the flower

language as slow and alien
in hues beget

     song

+

when walking was vicinity
in time
to be somewhere for someone
where the distance arrives

     smiles

+

and psalm beneath canopy tree
sways the way an eye does in passing

+

I visited a wood darker than paint
on a flat to represent night
here in a forest
cars and houses
food and the electric wire

tremble lights in squares
and a neighborhood

+

at the stem of my flank
a flower

as no human space

   open

(PROVIDENCE, MAY — AUGUST 1990)

III. Other Poems

Hours of the Book

For the longest time not so much as a going under, rather as a
singularly dark ascension into a remote neglected part of heaven.
— RAINER MARIA RILKE

Only in connection with a body does a shadow make sense.
— ROSMARIE WALDROP

MATINS

We can accept nothing
if there be not praise
of the word and light
to spade the page

This time:
a vault into which a god must not enter

Benign record
tracing the history
of a pulse from stone
Sweet contusion
taking only this blue swath
Where I go

The ornamental mind is feral

PRIME

The lesson of the disc
has not yet ascended into place

A statement:
"the oracle has been given"
is an event that bears no terms

to be a voice of an earth

The face of the one/the mask of the word
Intuition is given a name:
wreath circle and sphere

and the difficulty here
we cannot die
the difficulty

here is the full act

TERCE

Kindness is a trace element found
to be given in need. A cardinal
feather discovered in an ice-storm
from some distant March. There are paths
I have taken and then there is this walk,
an amend of earth and water is various
forever yielding an original gesture.
Words cannot color this. Learning
grace is composure of fear
out of care for the other, and
to repeat this say "Let us"
continue from here.

SEXT

Anger seeks a violent end

Glass broken against flesh
will not release this passion

The planet spins around the sun

Ellipse is the emblem of my decay
prayer the posture of wanting

Flight is invisible

unnecessary is invincible
while tolerance trends

Hands carry food on a tray

hunger seated indefinitely
Betrayal is sudden sharp

unfathomable

a ribcage a shoulder
blade

My clavicle is plumbago

NONES

Dear Miss Lonely Hearts
This condition of sky is terminal
It does not wend or want, dreams
Of an afternoon gaze
Are open, impenetrable
Like a sphinx, our wanting
Waits, wanting
Time, merely an impression
Worn upon the brow
My reach extends lives
To make of these hands

Monuments

VESPERS

Gentle vespers do not be sullen

tho sullen and sanguine
are your colors in cloud light

to have seen through the surface

of your words   proud beam
of a pilgrim heart   immigrant
mouth and brow   revealing

an exile's eyes: time kept

on a clock whose hands are breathing

COMPLINE

Saturn's window opens new lawns

In time there is understanding
for a widow's walk, mite and peak
This pain in the day's waxing
out of ken
                    Celestial
tremolo
            as offering

An elderly arm in a heat wave
is vulnerable or unexpected
news of illness at sundown
Dinner is over   The guests
have gone and you were not
among them
                    A place setting

removed in time is a pretense
This rationale—effusive

Forgiveness for a new moon

All we have is this sky
these trees and sleepless nights
There is a constellation I have
never seen   It consists of everyone
I love
        The portrait of

heaven keeps
on the face of a sundial

Nostos: Pro Patria

Abandoned beneath this sky
Without
Shades from a distance
We are
Watching sadly a 'Homecoming Queen'
Whose moment is over
Is there only nostalgia
For my hands remembering
A gesture
Remembering the telephone
And your voice
A long distance operator
And this poem abandoned
Miscellany & sky

Thirty Sentences for No One

It begins with socks in a drawer and continues to laundry bags to the future. In the Food Mart everything is above the child's head. Always looking up. Always lifting our eyes to heaven. The horizon is your mother's repose on the divan after daily chores. Outside rain repeats rain. I remember wanting hugs but was given food. I have grown into the sweater my aunt gave me. I was born on the third chapter of the novel forever asking what happened in the beginning. In the beginning sky. In the beginning earth. The aquarium is a prism at sunset in the library which articulates light on the spines as both a constant and ephemeral beauty. Come over to our house. I have grown into this sky I wear about my shoulders everywhere I am. The hamper in the mind is endless. Let me work my image into soil and treebark and leafstem. This is not who I remember. The first body was an environment a landmark on the frontier of tomorrow. The body of discourse is an apology of abuses and I am without reparation. In the meaning of the day the way one turns and looks—eyes for hands. Today the stranger the exile and spook are in my shaving mirror. In my dream you are real. I am as one who each day stands behind the tapestry and receives the needle to pull the thread taut and pass it back through. The design is no one's. Is there justice in every sentence? Then I read "death is not being unable to communicate but no longer being able to be understood" or something like that. Grass was the first species to cover the earth. I am incomplete. Indeed. All that was left is the state and the miles under my feet.

Psalm

No one lives there

X and delirium
—barely wider

than a sun

How many greater

than ourselves
is air

Feed the candle

the gate

and your house

Poem for John Wieners

I am not a poet
because I live in the actual world
where fear divides light
I have no protection against
the real evils and money
which is the world
where most lives are spent

I am not a poet
because I cannot sing about
lost kingdoms of righteousness
instead I see a woman in a blue parka
crying on the street today
without hope from despair

I am not a poet
for there is nothing I can say
in smart turns to deflect
oncoming blows of every day's
inexistence that creeps into
the contemporary horizon

I am not a poet
but a witness to bear the empty
space that becomes our hearts
if left to loiter or linger
without a life to share

I've seen sorrow on joy street
and heard the blur of the hurdy-gurdy
and I too know what evening means
but this is not real—poetry is
and from this have I partaken
as my eyes grow into the evolved dark

Postcard: I Hear America Singing

This is where an emblem goes
It is where you are
It says wish you were near
It says perfect picture
Says hopeful and dearest
It says thinking of you
In perfect hedge rows
With a broad expanse of water
With an immense rebuttal
Of space as here is where
Feeling grows
Vagrant naming and blue
It is 1:15 in providence
Dear Ted, hello!

Façades for Theron Ware

> He appears to the sudden house as if suspended.
> — KEITH WALDROP

I.

This photograph, mine, reproduces
exactly a state of exuberance
once remote and quite peaceful

as the window by the study, open
displays a world pleasant and
peopled. Even if from a distance

there are times when you discover
a purpose in life, without ever
trying to look for *illumination*.

II.

What was the novel telling, so
elegantly, about the young man
walking his way into a state

of grace? The way a refrain
repeats its thing and you
walk to the market, having

no memory of the entire score.
A cadence that bears no resemblance
to the actual rooms we enter.

III.

However variegated, repetition
exacts its tribute upon our
experience, sounding to the nape

of feeling; so often grace is mistaken
for this and we continue to move
through multitudes, to the one.

It has been written, then invented
or recorded, no matter, even
simple activity expires into song.

IV.

The heart hidden, or worn on
the surface, is contemptuous.
So going, you can't make up

your mind, as to wear a slicker
would permit rain. Ownership
bridles, remains illegitimate

and affords no grand finale.
The one you were looking for
over there. In letters.

v.

To restore the voice behind
an empty lot, and you strain
to recall a campfire's warmth.

They have all gone out with
the electric light. Indifferent
switch next to the nightstand.

An antique globe collecting
dust. These remedies maintaining
a kingdom. Or just overnight.

VI.

Reassurance, a cadenza:
this richness that grows as
the distance of a digression

increases feeling. Wandering
through ruins of a production
no longer staged is to experience

an anagnorisis unlike the real
thing. Here elaborations come
to play a surface into rapture.

VII.

She was walking a phantom line
an illiterate distance of a cloud's
plume against a mountain field.

Navigating from sidewalk to garden
path in the night. No explanation
was offered to demystify her passage.

The dream face was intact, also
beyond recollection, the same way
memory is unmistaken for memory.

VIII.

Farewell is a token we give or
take along this path of virtual
gates. To enter is to exit—for

going hence is arriving here. Grey
to grey. The actual landscape is
threshold. The way words are

only notes from an earlier caprice
of meaning. Know this by the lines
on your face, hands and throat.

IX.

It was a difficult beauty, tracing
a shadow cast from fragments
of broken narrative. I heard tell

of a man who asked for help, hanging
from a cliff face. A voice replied
"let go," as if faith were a free-

fall unto this couch. No matter
what I believe, the door to my head
will not open from the outside.

Often I Am Allowed These Messages

as if caught up in excess
that is the undoing
                    but the design

having been made
is mine

an entire other to sun
so that a limb extends

to an illiterate place
wherefrom a field unfolds

wherefrom this world insists
and I say
            the unimaginable distances

whose inscription remains
in the speed behind smiles
whose slippery light connects towns

and is a human power
                    this body

a conductor in an uninformed territory

whose banner displays a history
from an ineffable lexicon

often I am allowed these messages
as if the field could compose
that which arrives
                          out of nothing

everlasting proposition of sound

Dear Jack

There is a lot one might say
about love, manners or civic pride,
but let's not, and just
allow ourselves the silence.
Mourning doves between the houses
coo as our eyes reach to each other,
as our hearts dilate and slip
from the mantle we kept them on
and return to their original
but only more splendid for having
shattered long ago and now
seeming to triumph over the past.
What was the name of the place
you were hoping to visit and did you
want to stay or continue on
drunken to the next garden?
And say "here it is" or no "there
it is. I must be going." The heart
is capable to come to rest in one flag
or library or flower bed. Longer
than you care to consider. Do you
believe me? Am I telling the truth?
Our kisses are not truth or
the embodiment of higher ideals,
they are just
the simple exchange of being
here. Necessary as food. To continue
is the only contract I've signed
up to honor. So don't despair
if a little ink mixes in with my spittle.
It's there to remind us of the world,

inescapable like my hands and face
or your mouth. Is why I invent
this declaration, insisting on kisses,
and which I gladly vote for, Love.

Asserted Abundance

The traitors' handclaps were installed in the cubby of cloistered responses, meanwhile the statue of good deeds shone in the courtyard of the righteous. It seemed here was a dialogue to mend fences and span altered waters. Although religion had no place among the heretical claims of physical prodigies, its stamp authenticated the activities going on through years of cataclysm.

Who was going to end this discourse? was a question very much on the bystanders' downtrod faces and whitewashed spirit. So each was met with a ritual sacrifice, but still blood flowed with what seemed an immeasurable abundance from an unseen mover, and the accounts varied—even if the final tally remained odd.

Poetry like a proscription was nailed to the bloody rostra of new promise, as a single slender green sprout was recorded to have asserted itself in the crack of granite at the base of the old municipal building, from which all roads led. Some sucker growth of enthusiasm—stubborn and useless.

Recorded also, that its tenacious effort paled and the hordes were left to their spading, breaking macadam for food beneath the surface of the indifferent state. If ever a butterfly or song-bird was reported to have passed by, its arc was spread by word of mouth. So that the rumor of such marvel remained stitched in the seams of the workers' ragged overclothes.

Still Life with Automobile

He was going to take it to the next town.
Though the park was empty
the pond bristled with life. He had
not an answer within 100 sq. acres
or it was only answers that tweeted about.
Who was this lonely figure in a landscape
and once he is made known
would the narrative slack and come
to a warm bed and slippers?
It was no no and yes yes all afternoon
on the thruway. It was a big state said the signs
and so did the sky say big state.

A Speaking Part

It is that white stone
at the center of

a run of azure at its side
Here, you can displace it

Can you find the tiny smile
at the bottom of

in the basement of
A television and a flag

It broadcasts you, up there
a name evaporating

with its many colors gone

This sound travels too
in time

Will you know me
and bring the food you have

+

Back in the day

where the people are going someplace
where the buildings join in the distance—
decay of plant life and animal life—

     my nails are growing

The sounds far off are the sounds we make
in the great machine of government
the neighbor boy has made a friend

     to walk in the tall grass

Their little fists or flags—"Billy,
come home, Billy" the mother cries

+

Children uncover fear behind words

Behind meaning:
the grass and an empty lot
where men once worked

Behind this lot is a hill and a lake

They have been there
longer than the words that describe them

Sentences connect the child
the fear the lot the lake

but will connect us for no longer
than a nap, a nightmare, in the afternoon

where abandoned children hide
from the state

Children work hard to find meaning
behind the fear of the lot and the lake

Printed in the United Kingdom
by Lightning Source UK Ltd.
102394UKS00002BA/19